The First 25 Years Are the Hardest!

Other Ziggy Books

The First 25 Years Are the Hardest!

...a 25 Year Retrospective of ZiGGY'S Favorites by

Tom Wilson

ANDREWS and McMEEL
A Universal Press Syndicate Company
KANSAS CITY

ISBN: 0-8362-1033-6

Library of Congress Catalog Card Number: 95-80762

Life Happens
by Tom Wilson

Ziggy's upcoming 25th anniversary in syndication has prompted many readers to ask me, "Is it hard to come up with ideas for Ziggy, 365 days a year, year after year after year?" Because Ziggy so closely reflects what we're living, day after day, year after year, there will always be an idea for Ziggy. Life keeps happening. Ziggy is unique in the cartoon world because he is the only character who is doing what we're doing and dealing with what we're dealing with in our world. He commiserates with the reader and wrestles with the same troubles we are. And he celebrates the same simple pleasures we experience. And just as no one could have predicted smiley faces, mood rings, disco, sushi, and bad hair days, I never know what will happen to Ziggy until life happens to us.

It seems as though Ziggy has always been a part of my personal history. We've been together most of my life. I don't think I created Ziggy or invented him, it was more a case of acknowledging him. When I look back through much of my work done in 1968 B.Z. (Before Ziggy), I find him showing up in many humorous illustration drawings I had done. It wasn't until 1971, however, that I finally established his personality and he became known as Ziggy through the newspaper syndication.

I wanted Ziggy to be the little guy in the big world much like I felt as a kid. In fact, I've often said that growing up is a Ziggy experience, and one that I wouldn't care to repeat . . . so I made him clumsy and unsure, yet wide-eyed and full of wonder.

I wanted Ziggy to appeal to everyone, regardless of gender or generation, so I was careful to avoid specifics regarding age, occupation, background, etc.

I wanted him to be loved, so I designed him in somewhat rounded teddy bear proportions to make him more huggable. I wanted the readers not just to laugh at Ziggy, I wanted them to know him, to empathize with him, and of course, to enjoy him. To help achieve this, I tried in many of the daily panels to establish eye contact between Ziggy and the reader. My objective was to create an emotional rapport between Ziggy and his audience.

When Ziggy communicates, he connects with people. Ziggy speaks to us and for us in sharing our feelings. Whatever we want to express—humor, friendship, love, or good wishes—Ziggy says it in a way people respond to and remember.

The next 25 years? Like Ziggy, I have trouble looking too far ahead. (Maybe it has something to do with the size of our noses.) I see Ziggy evolving and changing with the times, as he always has, while still remaining the same lovable character he's always been. We've lately been thinking of launching Ziggy into cyberspace, but knowing Ziggy, he'd probably get tangled up in the Internet.

1971-1975

ZIG, YOU'RE A NICE GUY, BUT SUCH A SQUARE...LET ME ENLIGHTEN YOU ON JUST A FEW OF YOUR MISCONCEPTIONS...

HASH is NOT BEEF AND POTATOES
COOL is NOT A TEMPERATURE CONDITION
DOPE is NOT A DUMB PERSON AND
POT is NOT SOMETHING PEOPLE USED TO KEEP UNDER THE BED!!

...AND AS YOU KNOW, OUR GUESTS ON "SPEAK YOUR MIND" ARE MASKED TO PREVENT THEM FROM BEING ATTACKED BY ANGRY MOBS AS THEY LEAVE THE STUDIO...

THE ENERGY CRISIS... INFLATION...WATERGATE,... AND THE GENERAL STATE OF AFFAIRS, HAS BROUGHT THE COUNTRY CLOSER TOGETHER...

...MAKES US REALIZE THAT WE'RE ALL IN THE SAME BOAT.

....AND IT'S LEAKING !!

ONE GOOD THING ABOUT GETTING NO WHERE THESE DAYS IS..

...YOU CAN ALWAYS BLAME IT ON THE ENERGY CRISIS...

STREAKING IS JUST AN OBVIOUS MEANS OF GETTING ATTENTION

...I'D TRY IT MYSELF, BUT I'M AFRAID NOBODY WOULD NOTICE!!

FRIENDS ARE PEOPLE YOU LIKE,

...WHO LIKE YOU RIGHT BACK!!

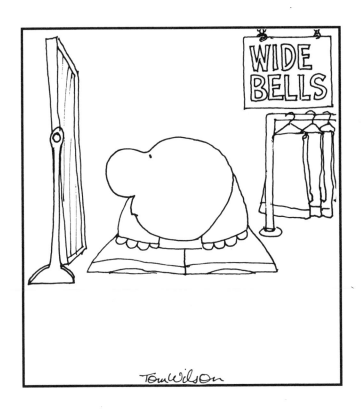

1976-1980

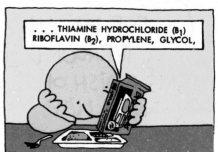

46

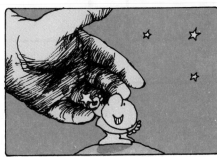

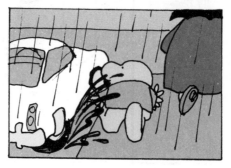

ZIGGY...

BY Tom Wilson

ZIGGY...
BY Tom Wilson

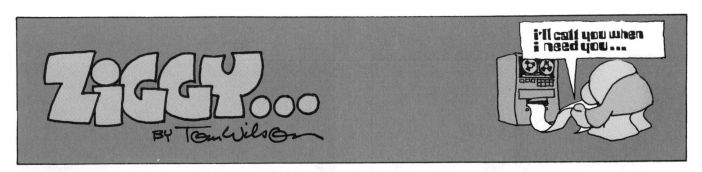

1981-1985

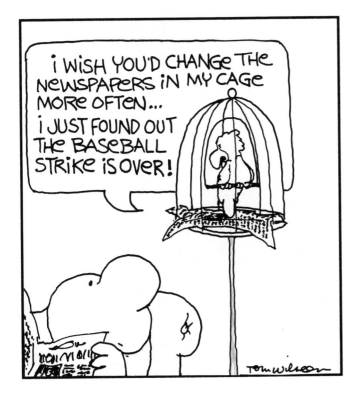

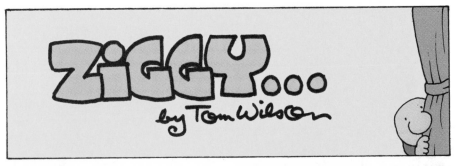

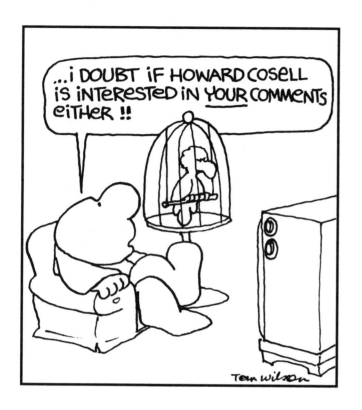

90

1986-1990

...BE REASONABLE, SIR. IF SOMEBODY GAVE YOU A CRUMMY TWENTY-TWO CENTS TO CARRY A LETTER ALL THE WAY TO ALTOONA ...HOW CAREFUL WOULD YOU BE?

POST OFFICE

Tom Wilson

Tom Wilson

ZiGGY...

by Tom Wilson

Tom Wilson

AFTER A WHILE I FIGURED OUT THAT I'VE GOT A LOT TO BE THANKFUL FOR!

I'VE GOT A NICE HOME, PETS THAT LOVE ME, ...ENOUGH TO EAT... HOBBIES...

I'M THANKFUL... SOMEWHERE ALONG THE WAY I STOPPED ANXIOUSLY WAITING FOR THINGS THAT I WANTED!

I GAVE UP WAITING AND JUST WENT ON LIVING... AND I DID ALL OF THE LITTLE THINGS I ENJOY...

I FIGURED THAT IF I COULDN'T BE HAPPY WITH WHAT I'VE GOT, THEN I'D NEVER BE HAPPY!

THEN A FUNNY THING HAPPENED...ONCE I ACCEPTED BEING CONTENT WITH WHAT I HAD...

... I STARTED TO GET THINGS I'D ALWAYS WANTED!

...LIKE CONTENTMENT AND HAPPINESS !!

108

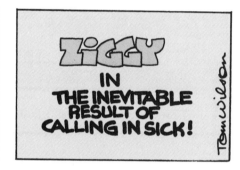

...i THINK i'VE BEEN GETTING **WAY** TOO MUCH JUNK MAIL LATELY! ...MY MAILBOX JUST THREW UP!

ZIGGY

LOOK, FUZZ, i REALIZE THAT ONE YEAR EQUALS SEVEN DOG YEARS, BUT WE'RE **STILL** ONLY GONNA CELEBRATE YOUR BIRTHDAY ONCE A YEAR!

ZIGGY by Tom Wilson

FERT

APRIL

MAY

SEED

JUNE

COUGH... GAG

JULY

AUGUST

SQUASH

TOMATOES

PEAS

SEPTEMBER   PRODUCE

124

HOME FOR DISCREDITED TELEVISION EVANGELISTS

...BOY, THE NEWS FROM THE MIDDLE EAST IS REALLY GETTING DEPRESSING! ...IT SEEMS LIKE IT'S JUST ONE "SADDAM" THING AFTER ANOTHER!

ZiGGY...
by Tom Wilson

HEY MOM! I'M HOME!!

1991-1995

IT WAS A GOOD SPEECH...BUT i THINK HE SHOULD HAVE SKIPPED THE "READ MY LIPS...NO MORE WARS" PART!

Ziggy... by Tom Wilson

HMMM!

CONTAINS: NO SALT, NO SUGAR, NO FAT, NO CHOLESTEROL, NO NITRATES, NO CALORIES...

NO ARTIFICIAL PRESERVATIVES NO ARTIFICIAL COLORING NO ARTIFICIAL SWEETENER...

NO ARTIFICIAL FLAVORS...

CHECKOUT

SUGAR PUFFIES

FROSTED YUKKIES

GOOFY POOFS

NO SALE!

137

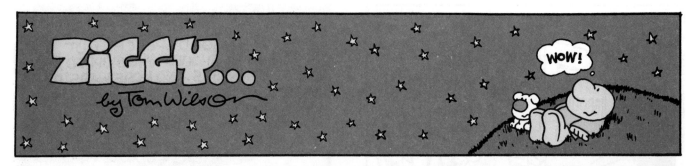

WOW!

...Y'KNOW FUZZ, THEY SAY THE UNIVERSE HAS BILLIONS OF STARS IN IT!!

...AND AROUND THOSE STARS COULD BE MANY MORE PLANETS! SOME OF THEM MIGHT EVEN BE ABLE TO SUPPORT LIFE!

...IT'S EVEN POSSIBLE THAT ONE OF THOSE BILLIONS OF PLANETS COULD BE VERY SIMILAR TO OUR PLANET!

...AND ON THAT PLANET, THERE MIGHT EVEN BE PEOPLE LIKE US!

...AND WHO KNOWS, AT THIS VERY MOMENT, ON A PLANET SOMEWHERE OUT THERE IN SPACE, PEOPLE VERY MUCH LIKE US ARE LOOKING UP AT THE STARS AND ARE WONDERING ABOUT THE SAME THINGS WE ARE!!

...NAAAAHH!!

NATIONAL ENDOWMENT FOR THE ART THAT NOBODY IS WILLING TO PAY FOR

THIS IS CHUCK GENTILE IN WHAT USED TO BE THE SOVIET UNION... WE NOW SWITCH YOU TO ALEX SZABO IN WHAT USED TO BE YUGOSLAVIA!!

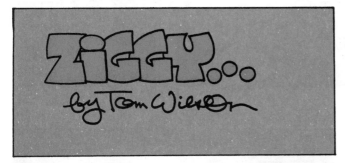

... *to be continued...*